Baptism and Chrismation

FATHER JOHN & HOLY PIMOLY EXPLAIN IT ALL!

in the Coptic Orthodox Church

BY FATHER GREGORY BISHAY & JOSEPH GERGES
LAYOUT BY: ASHRAF IBRAHIM

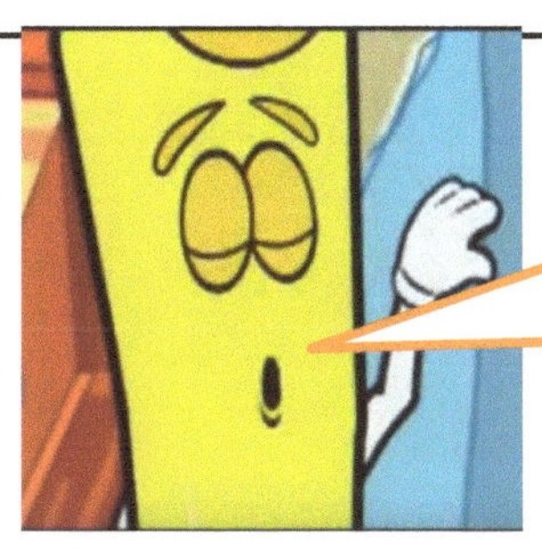

Father John, what is baptism?

What a great question Moe! Baptism is *being born from heaven*! That's why Saint Paul says "we were *buried with Him* through baptism into death, that just as Christ was raised from the dead by the glory of the Father, even so we also should walk in newness of life."

You probably don't know a whole lot about your baptism because you were a baby when your parents baptized you! But don't worry, Moe. Let's learn about your baptism and explain what it all means!

Originally, the word baptism meant *to dye* like what happens to clothes. Just like shirts start out one color and ends up a different color, baptism *changes* the way a person looks *from the inside*, not the outside! We also believe that baptism is the *door to Christianity!* We change and become *new* children of God!

That reminds me that we read about the baptism of our Lord Jesus in the *gospels* of Saint Mark, John and Luke!

You're right Moe! Back 2,000 years ago *John the Baptist* baptized our Lord Jesus in the *Jordan river* to set an *example for us!* Let's take a look at how it happened...

I need to be baptized by you Lord, and *you are coming to me?!*

Permit it to be so now, for thus it is fitting for us to fulfill *all righteousness*.

For Parents and Servants: This book is intended for children ages 8-11 (3rd – 5th grades). It is the first of a series of books teaching the mysteries (sacraments) of the Church. Among the goals of this book are to introduce: (i) the concept of baptism and Chrismation (Myron) and its necessity for being a Christian; (ii) key Biblical verses about baptism and (iii) the importance of following the example set by the Lord and His direct teaching.

He was *fully immersed* in the Jordan river in His baptism. And as we'll learn *we do the same thing!*

And when He came up from the water, a *dove* descended on Him! This was the *Holy Spirit* in dove form!

And a voice was heard from heaven saying " *This is my beloved Son in whom I am well pleased!*" We call this an *Epiphany* because the *Holy Trinity* appeared: the *Father* (the voice), the *Son* (Jesus) and the *Holy Spirit* (the dove)!

Do you know why Jesus was baptized in a river? To set an example for us!

He taught us to be baptized in *water* and *Spirit!* Just like the Holy Spirit on the Jordan River!

This is the *mystery* of Baptism! It has the power to transform the water and make us born again!

A mystery?! Like a detective story?

No, Moe. A mystery is the *invisible way* the Holy Spirit gives a material heavenly power through the blessings of a priest. We also call it a *sacrament* too.

Just like how the Holy Spirit and the prayers of the priest *gives power* to the water in baptism so that we can *die* with Christ and be *reborn* with Him! Let me show you...

Here comes the priest getting the water ready for baptism. He starts by *blessing the water* with special prayers. He also blesses it *oil!*

Like oils from the grocery store?

Corn Oil
Canola Oil
olive OIL

No, Moe. These are *specially blessed* holy oils by the Church!

There are *three kinds of oil* used by the Church during baptism! Let's learn about them...

HOLY OIL
This is regular *holy oil* that has been blessed by the Church!

GALILAWEN OIL
And this is the *galilawen oil*. It is the *oil of joy*!

HOLY OIL
CHRISMATION OIL
GALILAWEN OIL
Finally, this is the *Chrismation* oil. It is also called the *Myron oil*. It is the oil that makes you a Christian!

The priest uses these oils and, through the *mystery* of baptism, the oils *transform* the baby into a new child of heaven!
Like a magic potion? Will it change the water into a car?

No, Moe. That's why we call it a *mystery* or a *sacrament!* We can't see *how,* but the prayers and the oil give the water *heavenly power!* It gives the baby a *new birth!*

Did you know Moe that there were *other symbols* of baptism in the Bible?
Really? Tell me about them!

One *symbol of baptism is* Noah's Ark! Just like the ark saved Noah and the animals from the *storm* and give them a new life, so does baptism! It gives us a *new life with God!*

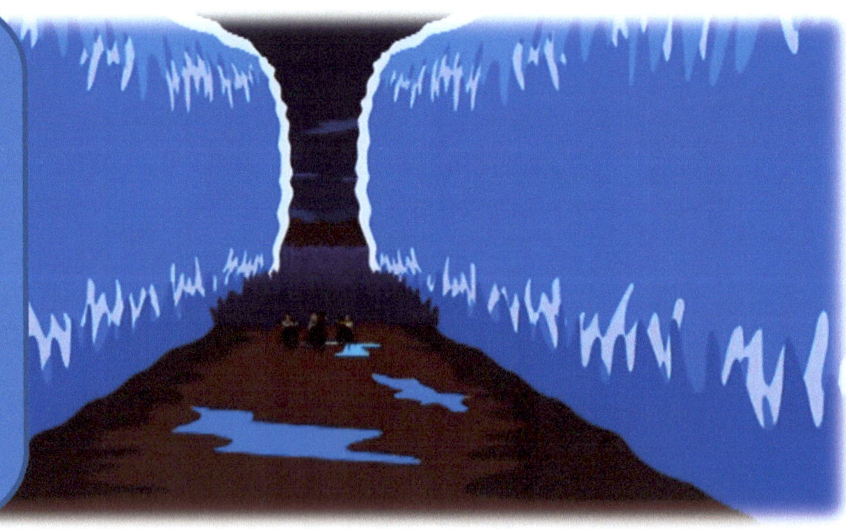

Another symbol is the Israelites *passing through the Red Sea* to get to the *promised land!* The water *saved* them by drowning the *Egyptians* perusing them! So, baptism *saves us* by removing the devil's power and giving us a *new nature!*

But nobody drowns in baptism!

It's a different kind of death Moe! The priest dips us all into the water to *kill* our *old man* that was *corrupted* and we are reborn with a *new nature!*

Right Moe! That was in *Colossians* 2:12 and *Romans* 6:4

And the Apostle Paul says that we are *buried* with Christ in baptism and *resurrected* with Him to a new life!

So you see how important the baptism is Moe? It is the way that *kill the old person* and are *reborn from heaven* with *water* and the *Holy Spirit!* That's why we can say that the baptismal basin is where a life *begins* and a life *ends!*

Now let's go back to the baptismal room to see what happens after the priest has blessed the water...

After the priest blesses the water, there's a special prayer for the mother called the *absolution of the mother.* Then, the baby being baptized as to accept the faith!

How can a baby accept the faith? He can't talk yet!

The parents do it for him! The parents commit to the faith of the Church and to teaching the baby when he grows!

They first turn to the *west* and *denounce* Satan and all his evil, then they turn to the *east* and accept Christ, the faith of the Church and His resurrection! They do this for the baby, but if the person being baptized is an adult, then he would *accept the faith* himself!
WEST

EAST

Then the priest dips the baby *completely* in the water *three times* saying "I baptize you John in the name of the *Father,* and the *Son* and the *Holy Spirit*". He gives the baby a new Christian name!

On the mountain in Galilee, Jesus told his disciples: "Go therefore and make disciples of all nations, baptizing them in the name of the Father and of the Son and of the Holy Spirit. And Lo, I am with you always, even until the end of the age."

He actually told us what to do and showed us how to do it! On the mountain Jesus said the words, and in the Jordan river He immersed Himself in the water.
But baptism only *prepares* a person to receive the Holy Spirit. Actually receiving the Holy Spirit is another mystery right after baptism. It's called the *Holy Chrismation* where the priest anoints with the holy *Chrismation oil!*

The priest anoints the baby *36 times* with the holy Chrismation oil!

He anoints the forehead, the eyes, the nose, the ears and the mouth! All in the shape of a cross! This protects and anoints the baby's *mind and senses!*

He then anoints heart and the belly.

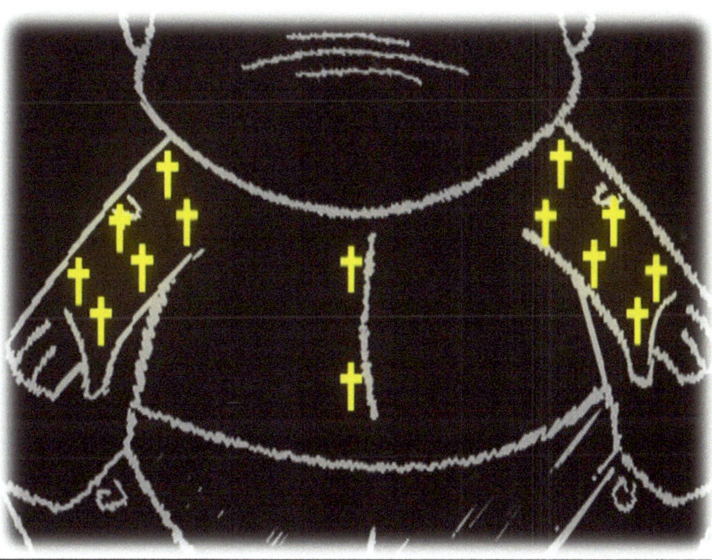

Then the priest anoints the baby's back and arms. This protects and consecrates all the *baby's will and actions*!

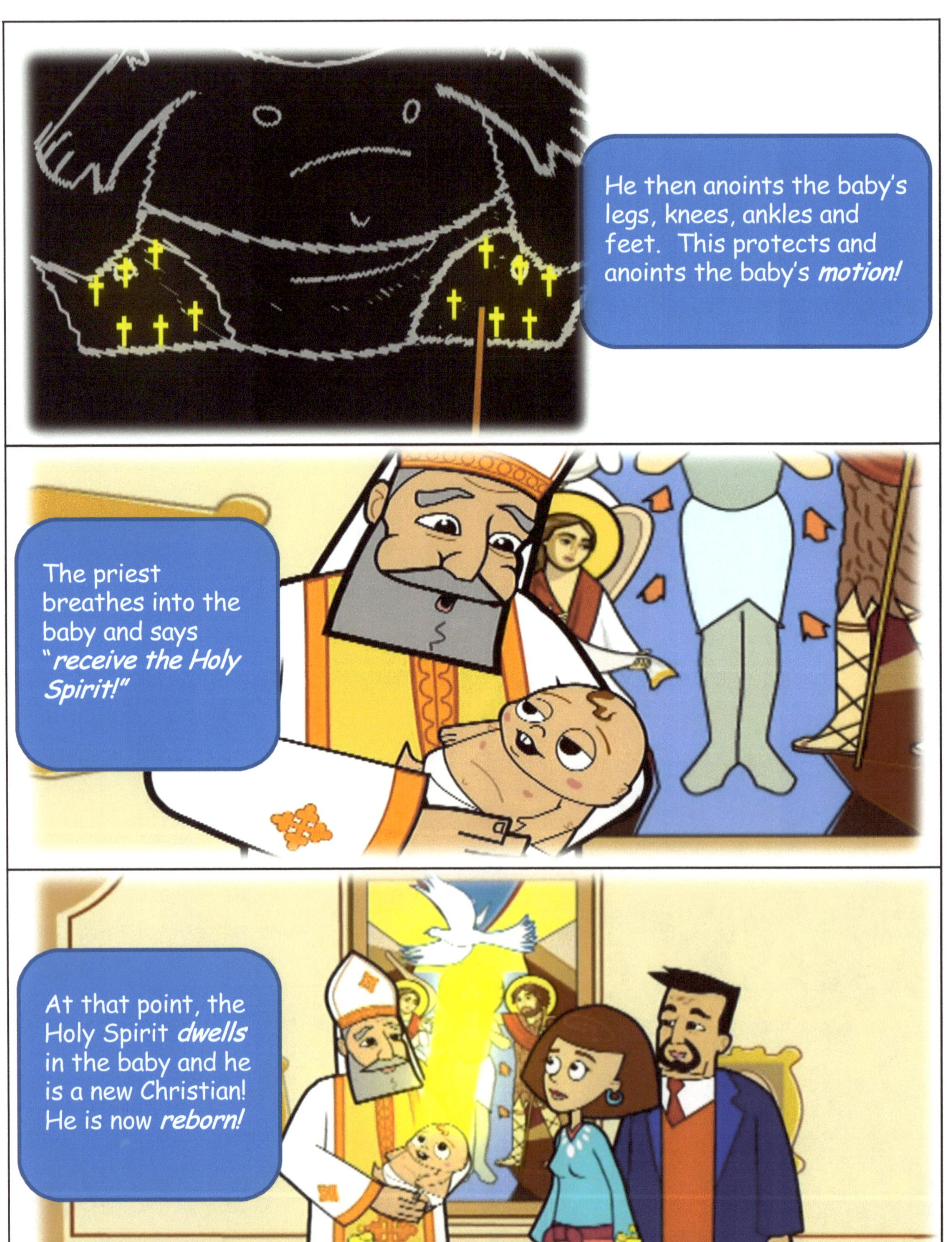
He then anoints the baby's legs, knees, ankles and feet. This protects and anoints the baby's motion!
The priest breathes into the baby and says "receive the Holy Spirit!"
At that point, the Holy Spirit dwells in the baby and he is a new Christian! He is now reborn!

Now that the baby is a new Christian, we put him in *new clothes, a red ribbon and a crown!*
The new white gown is his *purity*! And the crown is his *royalty* as a son of Jesus the King! The ribbon is red *like the blood of Christ!*

Our new Christian is now ready to receive his *first communion*—the *mystery of the Eucharist!*

Baptism and Chrismation in the Coptic Orthodox Church

Workbook

By Father Gregory Bishay & Joseph Gerges

Are you ready for some *questions* to see what you've learned? OK—here's an easy one: what did the word *baptism* originally mean and how does this relate to us?

Do you know where our Lord Jesus was *baptized?* And who baptized him?

Do you know what we *call* the baptism of Jesus?
What did the *voice from heaven* say when Jesus was baptized?

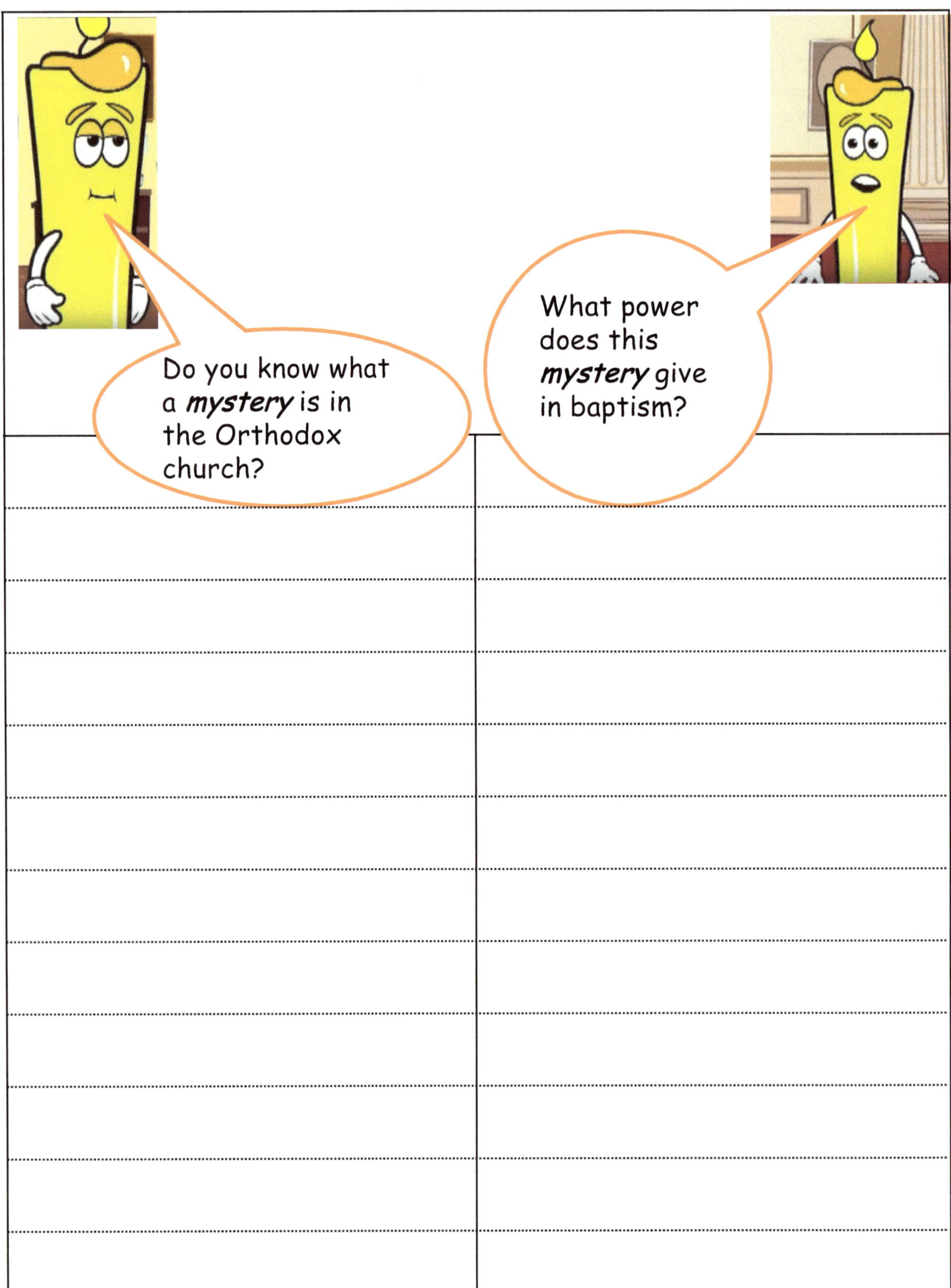
Do you know what a *mystery* is in the Orthodox church?
What power does this *mystery* give in baptism?

I learned about *oils* used in baptism! And they're not like grocery store oils! Can you *name the oils* used in baptism?
Corn Oil
Canola Oil
olive OIL

Can you names some *symbols of baptism* from the bible and *how they are like baptism?*

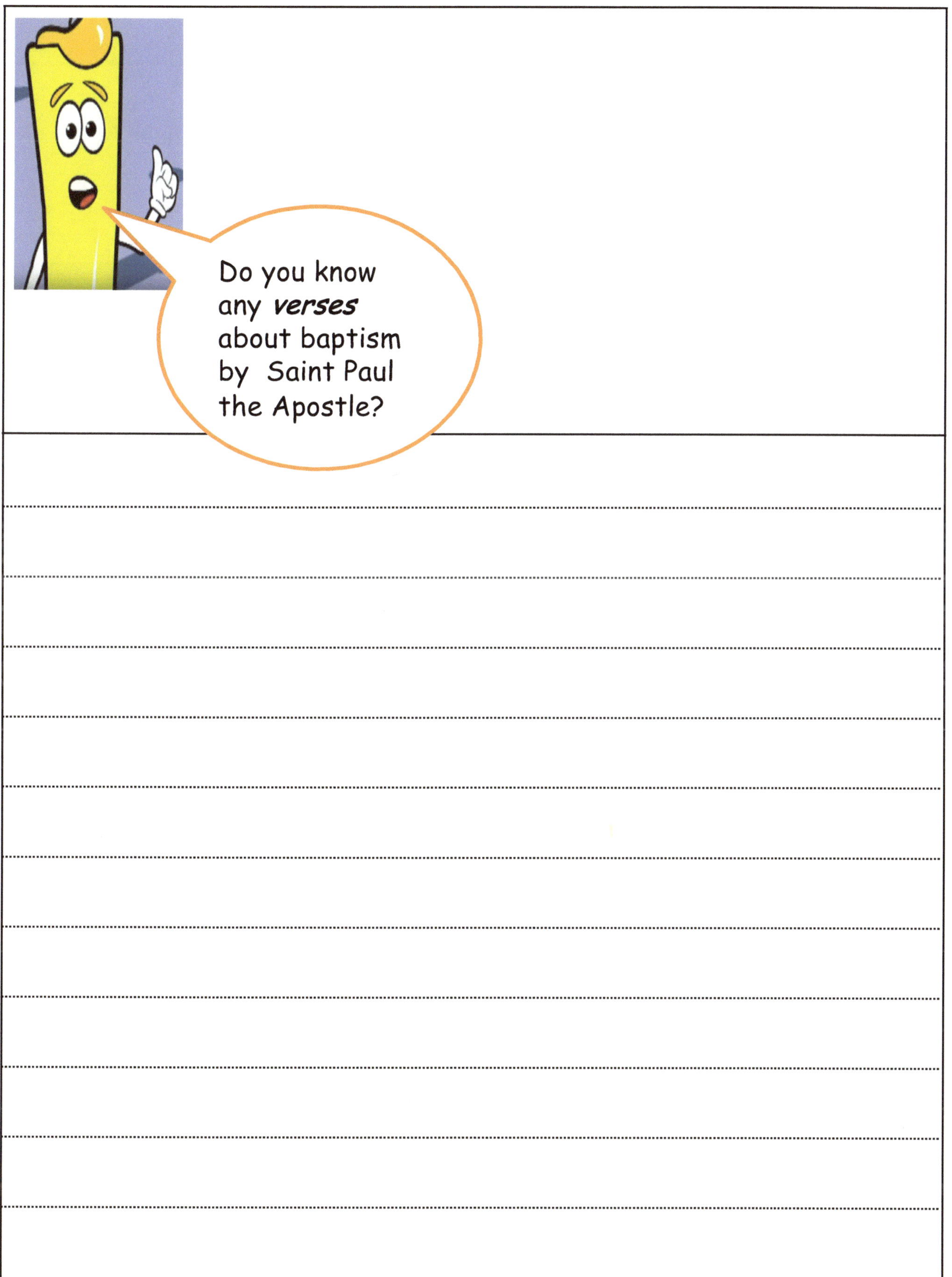
Do you know
any *verses*
about baptism
by Saint Paul
the Apostle?

Do you know what the *parents* do when they turn to the *east* and *west* during baptism?
WEST
EAST

Do you know what the priest *says* when he *dips the baby in the water?*

What did *Jesus say* about *how to baptize* to his disciples?

Do you know what the mystery of *receiving the Holy Spirit* is called?

How many times does the priest *anoint* the baptized with the holy Chrismation oil?

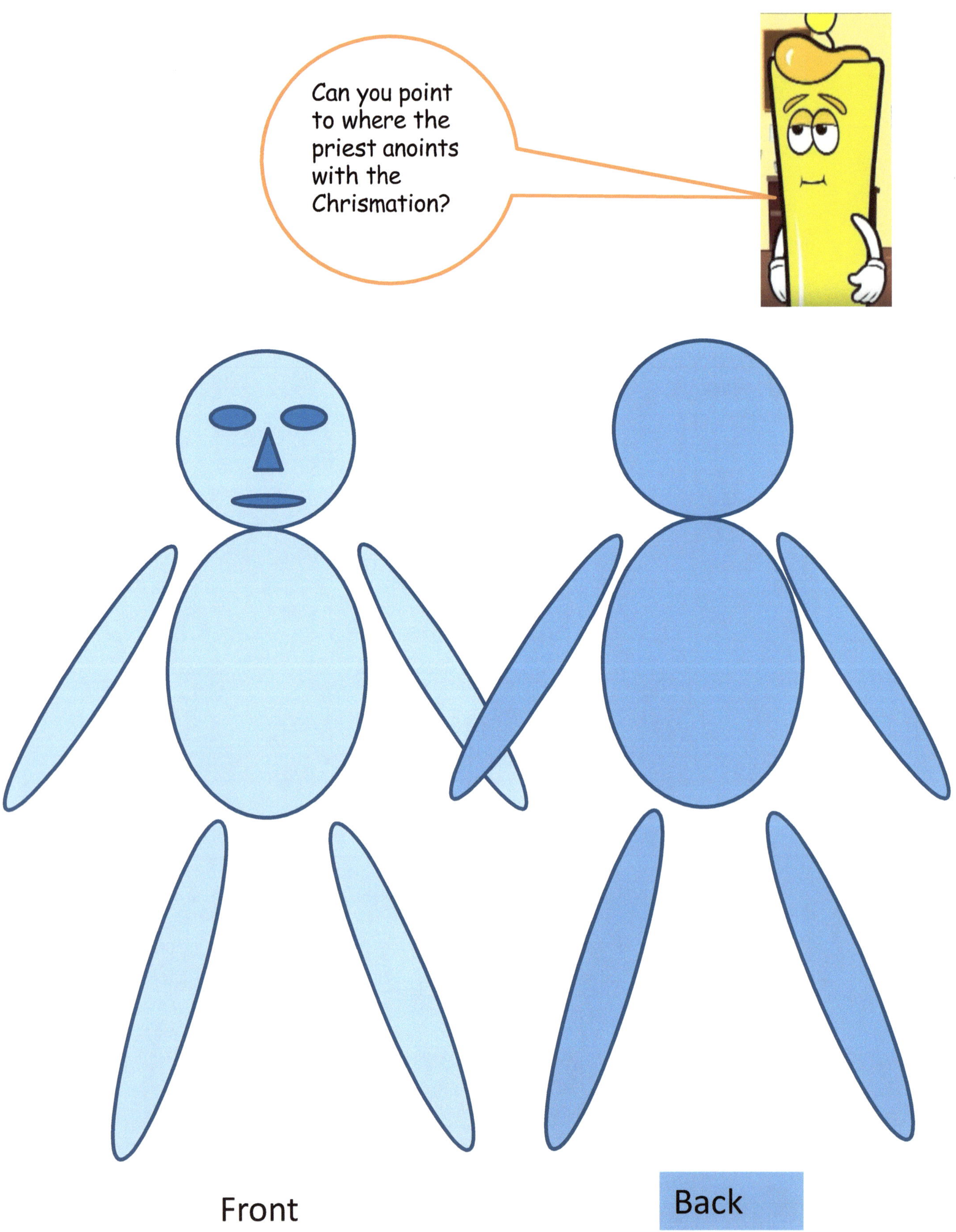

Can you point to where the priest anoints with the Chrismation?
Front
Back

What happens next?

After the anointing do you know what the priest does to the baby?

What *three items* are put in the baptized and what do they symbolize?

Do you know *what mystery comes after* the Chrismation and the dwelling of the Holy Spirit?